Empower Yourself Against Cyber Crimes and Frauds

C. P. Kumar
Reiki Healer
Roorkee - 247667, India

Disclaimer

While every effort has been made to ensure the accuracy and completeness of the content in this book, the author cannot guarantee that the information contained herein is error-free, up-to-date, or suitable for every individual circumstance.

The author shall not be held liable or responsible for any errors or omissions in the content of the book, nor for any damages, or losses that may arise from any actions taken based upon the suggestions or contents presented in the book.

Readers are advised to use their own judgment and discretion in applying the information provided in this book, and to consult with qualified professionals before taking any action based on the contents of this book. The author disclaims any and all liability or responsibility for any actions taken or not taken based on the information contained in this book.

DEDICATION

To all individuals who strive to protect themselves and their communities from the insidious dangers lurking in the digital realm,

This book is dedicated to you.

In a world increasingly interconnected by technology, where the boundaries between physical and virtual spaces blur, the threat of cyber crimes and frauds looms large. It is a battle fought not with swords and shields, but with knowledge and vigilance. It is a battle that requires each one of us to be empowered, informed, and prepared.

To those who have fallen victim to cyber criminals, this dedication is a reminder that you are not alone. Your experiences have fueled our determination to shed light on the dark corners of the digital world, to unravel the intricate webs spun by those who seek to exploit our vulnerabilities.

To the tireless researchers and experts who have dedicated their lives to understanding and countering cyber threats, your unwavering commitment to safeguarding our digital lives has inspired us. This dedication is a testament to your invaluable contributions.

To the brave individuals who have spoken out against cyberstalking, harassment, and bullying, you have shown us the strength that lies within, even in the face of adversity. Your resilience has laid the foundation for change, and this dedication honors your courage.

To the legislators and policymakers who are tirelessly working to forge a legal framework that keeps pace with the ever-evolving nature of cyber crimes, this dedication recognizes your efforts. Your commitment to justice and the protection of society is indispensable.

And finally, to every reader who holds this book in their hands, seeking knowledge and guidance, we dedicate this work to you. It is our hope that within these pages, you will find the tools to empower yourself against cyber crimes and frauds. May you navigate the digital landscape with confidence, armed with the knowledge to protect yourself and those around you.

With utmost respect and gratitude,

C. P. Kumar

CONTENTS

PREFACE

In our increasingly interconnected and digital world, the threat of cyber crimes and frauds looms larger than ever before. The rapid advancements in technology have brought numerous benefits, but they have also opened the floodgates to malicious actors seeking to exploit vulnerabilities for personal gain. From phishing attacks to data breaches, cyberstalking to online scams, the range and complexity of these threats continue to evolve, leaving individuals and organizations vulnerable.

This book, "Empower Yourself Against Cyber Crimes and Frauds," aims to equip readers with the knowledge and tools necessary to navigate the treacherous waters of the digital realm. By understanding the techniques employed by cyber criminals and fraudsters, individuals can fortify their defenses, protect their identities, and safeguard their digital lives.

The book begins with an introductory chapter that provides an overview of cyber crimes and frauds, highlighting their prevalence and impact on society. It sets the stage for the subsequent chapters, which delve into specific aspects of the cyber threat landscape.

Readers will gain insights into the modern cyber threat landscape and the tactics employed by cyber criminals. The chapters that follow shed light on deceptive techniques used in phishing attacks and provide prevention strategies to counter them effectively. Identity theft, one of the most prevalent cyber crimes, is explored, offering readers guidance on unmasking digital imposters.

The human element is often exploited in cyber crimes, and the book addresses this issue through an examination of social engineering techniques. It further explores the realm of online scams, ranging from romance to investment frauds, exposing the tactics used and empowering readers to detect and avoid falling victim to these fraudulent schemes.

Malware attacks have become increasingly sophisticated, and the book provides valuable insights into how vulnerabilities are exploited for profit. Additionally, it tackles the growing menace of ransomware and offers defense mechanisms to thwart these attacks effectively. The importance of protecting sensitive information is emphasized in the chapter on data breaches, where readers will learn about the potential consequences and methods for safeguarding their personal and organizational data.

Financial frauds have plagued the digital world, and the book unravels the complex web of deception surrounding these crimes. It also addresses cyberstalking and harassment, shedding light on methods to protect personal privacy in the face of relentless digital intrusion. Cyberbullying, another distressing reality, is explored, providing guidance on navigating the digital abuse terrain.

Intriguingly, the book delves into the hidden underbelly of the internet, the dark web, revealing its mysteries and shedding light on the criminal activities that take place in its depths. While this section serves as a cautionary tale, it also underscores the importance of remaining vigilant in an increasingly interconnected world.

Practical guidance on implementing cybersecurity best practices is offered, enabling readers to proactively safeguard their digital lives. The book also explores the legal framework that surrounds cyber crimes and frauds, highlighting the battle being waged to bring perpetrators to justice.

Finally, the book looks toward the future, exploring emerging threats and technological safeguards. By staying informed about the ever-evolving landscape of cyber crimes, readers will be better prepared to anticipate and mitigate future threats.

Through comprehensive research and expert insights, this book aims to empower individuals, organizations, and communities to take a proactive stance against cyber crimes and frauds. By understanding the strategies and techniques employed by cyber criminals and fraudsters, readers will be armed with the knowledge to protect themselves and those around them.

Now, let us embark on this journey together, arming ourselves with the knowledge and tools needed to empower ourselves against cyber crimes and frauds.

C. P. Kumar
Reiki Healer
Former Scientist 'G', National Institute of Hydrology
Roorkee - 247667, India
E-mail: cpkumar@yahoo.com
Web: https://www.angelfire.com/nh/cpkumar/virgo.html

Introduction

In today's digital age, technology has transformed our lives in countless ways, making our lives easier and more interconnected than ever before. However, with the advantages of the digital world come significant risks and challenges. Cyber crimes and frauds have become a pervasive threat, posing serious implications for individuals, businesses, and governments worldwide. This article provides an overview of cyber crimes and frauds, shedding light on their nature, types, and the impact they have on our society.

Defining Cyber Crimes

Cyber crimes refer to criminal activities that are carried out through digital devices and the internet. These crimes exploit technological vulnerabilities to gain unauthorized access, steal data, disrupt systems, and commit fraudulent activities. They encompass a wide range of unlawful acts committed in cyberspace.

Types of Cyber Crimes

There are various types of cyber crimes that criminals engage in. Some common forms include:

1. Hacking and Unauthorized Access

This involves gaining unauthorized access to computer systems or networks with the intention of stealing information, disrupting operations, or causing harm.

2. Identity Theft

Identity theft occurs when someone steals another person's personal information, such as their name, Social Security number, or credit card details, to commit fraud or other criminal activities.

3. Phishing and Social Engineering

Phishing involves tricking individuals into revealing sensitive information by posing as a trustworthy entity, often through deceptive emails or fake websites. Social engineering tactics manipulate people into providing confidential information or performing actions that benefit the attacker.

4. Malware and Ransomware Attacks

Malware refers to malicious software designed to disrupt, damage, or gain unauthorized access to computer systems. Ransomware encrypts victims' data, holding it hostage until a ransom is paid.

5. Online Fraud and Scams

Online fraud includes various deceptive schemes, such as online shopping scams, lottery scams, romance scams, and investment frauds, aimed at defrauding individuals or businesses for financial gain.

Impacts of Cyber Crimes and Frauds

1. Financial Losses

Cyber crimes and frauds result in substantial financial losses for individuals, businesses, and governments. The costs incurred include stolen funds, recovery expenses, legal fees, and reputational damage.

2. Data Breaches and Privacy Violations

Data breaches compromise sensitive information, including personal and financial data, leading to privacy violations and potential identity theft. Such breaches erode trust in organizations and can have far-reaching consequences for individuals affected.

3. Disruption of Services

Cyber attacks can disrupt critical services, such as power grids, transportation systems, or healthcare facilities. This poses risks to public safety and can cause widespread chaos and economic damage.

4. Psychological and Emotional Impact

Victims of cyber crimes often experience significant psychological distress, including anxiety, fear, and a loss of trust in technology. The emotional toll can be long-lasting and impact personal well-being.

Combating Cyber Crimes and Frauds

1. Legislative Measures

Governments around the world have enacted legislation to address cyber crimes and frauds. These laws define cyber crimes, establish legal frameworks, and prescribe penalties for offenders. Law enforcement agencies work to enforce these laws and bring cyber criminals to justice.

2. International Cooperation

Given the transnational nature of cyber crimes, international cooperation is crucial. Countries collaborate through mutual legal assistance treaties and information-sharing platforms to investigate cyber crimes, track down criminals, and share best practices in combating cyber threats.

3. Cybersecurity Measures

Organizations and individuals must adopt robust cybersecurity measures to protect themselves from cyber crimes. This includes implementing firewalls, using strong passwords, regularly updating software, and educating users about potential threats.

4. Awareness and Education

Raising awareness about cyber crimes and frauds is vital to empower individuals and businesses to recognize and mitigate potential risks. Educational programs, workshops, and public campaigns play a crucial role in promoting cybersecurity awareness and best practices.

The Future of Cyber Crimes and Frauds

The landscape of cyber crimes and frauds continues to evolve rapidly as technology advances. Criminals are constantly finding new methods to exploit vulnerabilities and bypass security measures. Emerging technologies like artificial intelligence and the Internet of Things introduce additional challenges and risks. As a result, it is essential for individuals, organizations, and governments to remain vigilant, adapt to the changing threat landscape, and invest in robust cybersecurity strategies.

Conclusion

As our society becomes increasingly interconnected, the prevalence of cyber crimes and frauds continues to grow. Understanding the nature and impact of these crimes is crucial to protect ourselves and our digital assets. By staying informed, adopting strong security measures, and promoting cybersecurity awareness, we can mitigate the risks posed by cyber criminals and create a safer digital environment for all.

Introduction

In today's interconnected world, where technology plays an increasingly vital role, the cyber threat landscape has evolved into a complex and pervasive challenge. From individual users to large corporations and even governments, everyone is susceptible to cyber threats. This article aims to shed light on the modern cyber threat landscape, exploring its various dimensions and offering insights into the nature of these threats.

The Expanding Cyber Threat Landscape

The cyber threat landscape has expanded exponentially in recent years, driven by the proliferation of connected devices, cloud computing, and the growing interdependence of digital systems. Hackers and cybercriminals now have a wider attack surface, targeting not only traditional computer systems but also smartphones, IoT devices, and critical infrastructure. This expanding landscape poses a significant challenge for individuals and organizations alike.

The Motivations Behind Cyber Attacks

Understanding the motivations behind cyber attacks is crucial in comprehending the modern threat landscape. While financial gain remains a primary motive for many cybercriminals, there are other factors at play. Nation-states engage in cyber warfare to gain political leverage, gather intelligence, or disrupt adversaries' operations. Hacktivist groups aim to promote social or political causes by targeting organizations aligned with opposing ideologies. Additionally, some attacks are driven by curiosity, thrill-seeking, or personal vendettas.

Common Cyber Threats

1. Malware: **Malicious** software, such as viruses, worms, and ransomware, poses a significant threat. These programs exploit vulnerabilities in systems, compromise data integrity, and can cause financial losses or disruptions in critical services.

2. Phishing: **Phishing** attacks attempt to deceive users into revealing sensitive information, often through emails, messages, or fake websites. These attacks prey on human vulnerability and can lead to identity theft or financial fraud.

3. Distributed Denial of Service (DDoS): **DDoS** attacks overwhelm targeted systems with a flood of traffic, rendering them inaccessible to legitimate users. These attacks can disrupt online services, impact revenue, and damage reputations.

4. Insider Threats: **Employees** or insiders with malicious intent can pose a significant risk to organizations. They may leak sensitive data, sabotage systems, or provide unauthorized access to cybercriminals.

5. Advanced Persistent Threats (APTs): **APTs** are sophisticated and prolonged attacks, often backed by nation-states. They involve stealthy infiltration, long-term persistence, and data exfiltration. APTs can cause extensive damage, compromising national security or corporate secrets.

Evolving Techniques and Tactics

Cybercriminals constantly adapt their techniques and tactics to stay one step ahead. They exploit zero-day vulnerabilities, employ social engineering tactics, use encryption to evade detection, and leverage AI and machine learning to automate attacks. Additionally, the rise of the dark web has facilitated the sale of hacking tools, stolen data, and hacking-for-hire services, further fueling the sophistication of modern cyber threats.

The Impact of Cyber Threats

Cyber threats have far-reaching consequences for individuals, organizations, and societies as a whole. Financial losses from data breaches and ransom demands can be crippling for businesses. Personal information breaches lead to identity theft and compromised privacy. Attacks on critical infrastructure, such as power grids or transportation systems, can disrupt essential services and pose risks to public safety. Moreover, the erosion of trust in digital systems and the constant fear of cyber attacks can have psychological and societal impacts.

Mitigating the Modern Cyber Threats

1. Robust Security Measures: Implementing strong security measures, including firewalls, antivirus software, and intrusion detection systems, is essential for protecting against known threats.

2. Regular Updates and Patching: Keeping software and systems up to date with the latest patches helps address vulnerabilities and protect against known exploits.

3. User Education and Awareness: Educating individuals about cyber threats, promoting safe online practices, and teaching them to identify phishing attempts can significantly reduce the risk of successful attacks.

4. Incident Response and Recovery Plans: Organizations should develop robust incident response plans to effectively manage cyber incidents and minimize the impact of attacks. Regular backups of critical data are also vital for recovery.

5. Collaboration and Information Sharing: Public-private partnerships and information sharing initiatives help disseminate threat intelligence, identify emerging patterns, and collectively strengthen cyber defenses.

Conclusion

The modern cyber threat landscape is dynamic and pervasive, constantly evolving with new techniques and motivations. To counter this ever-present risk, individuals and organizations must remain vigilant, adapt their security measures, and stay informed about emerging threats. By understanding the nature of cyber threats, implementing robust security measures, and fostering collaboration, we can collectively build a safer digital environment for everyone.

Introduction

In today's digital age, where technology plays a central role in our lives, cybercriminals are continuously finding new ways to exploit unsuspecting individuals and organizations. One such method is phishing, a deceptive technique used to trick people into revealing sensitive information, such as passwords, credit card details, or personal data. This article explores the various tactics employed by cybercriminals in phishing attacks and provides effective prevention strategies to stay safe in the digital realm.

Understanding Phishing Attacks

Phishing attacks typically involve the use of fraudulent emails, text messages, or websites that impersonate legitimate entities, such as banks, social media platforms, or online retailers. The goal is to deceive individuals into taking specific actions, such as clicking on malicious links, opening infected attachments, or divulging personal information.

Common Phishing Techniques

1. Email Spoofing

Email spoofing is a prevalent phishing technique where cybercriminals forge the "From" field of an email to make it appear as if it originated from a trustworthy source. They often use recognizable logos, email addresses, and professional language to gain credibility and trick users into responding to their requests.

2. Spear Phishing

Spear phishing is a targeted attack where cybercriminals personalize their messages and tailor them to specific individuals or organizations. They gather information about their targets from various sources, such as social media, to make the messages appear legitimate and increase the chances of success.

3. Clone Websites

Cybercriminals create clone websites that closely resemble popular and trusted platforms, such as banking portals or e-commerce websites. These fraudulent websites aim to trick users into entering their login credentials or financial information, which the attackers then exploit for malicious purposes.

4. Smishing

Smishing, a combination of "SMS" and "phishing," involves phishing attacks conducted through text messages. Attackers send fraudulent messages with enticing offers or urgent requests, prompting recipients to click on malicious links or provide sensitive information via reply.

Prevention Strategies

1. Awareness and Education

Promoting awareness and providing education on phishing attacks is crucial in the fight against cybercrime. Individuals and organizations should stay informed about the latest phishing techniques, including email and website spoofing, and understand the potential risks involved.

2. Verify the Sender

Before responding to any email or text message, it is essential to verify the sender's authenticity. Pay close attention to email addresses, URLs, and domain names. Contact the organization directly through trusted channels to confirm the legitimacy of the message.

3. Exercise Caution with Links and Attachments

Avoid clicking on suspicious links or downloading attachments from unknown sources. Hover over hyperlinks to reveal the actual destination URL, and be cautious of shortened links, as they can mask malicious websites. Additionally, scan attachments with reputable antivirus software before opening them.

4. Strengthen Passwords and Enable Two-Factor Authentication

Use strong, unique passwords for each online account and avoid reusing them. Enable two-factor authentication whenever possible to add an extra layer of security. Two-factor authentication requires users to provide an additional verification method, such as a unique code sent to their mobile device, along with their password.

5. Keep Software and Systems Updated

Regularly update operating systems, web browsers, and security software to ensure protection against the latest vulnerabilities and phishing techniques. Enable automatic updates whenever possible to stay up to date with the latest security patches.

6. Use Anti-Phishing Tools and Software

Utilize anti-phishing tools and software that can identify and block suspicious websites and emails. These tools often include features like email filtering, link scanners, and real-time threat detection, enhancing your defense against phishing attacks.

7. Report Phishing Attempts

If you receive a phishing email, report it to the appropriate organization, such as the Anti-Phishing Working Group (APWG) or the Federal Trade Commission (FTC). Reporting phishing attempts helps authorities track and take action against cybercriminals, protecting others from falling victim to similar attacks.

Conclusion

Phishing attacks continue to pose a significant threat to individuals and organizations alike. By understanding the deceptive techniques employed by cybercriminals and implementing effective prevention strategies, we can minimize the risk of falling victim to phishing attacks. Stay vigilant, exercise caution when dealing with unsolicited requests for personal information, and prioritize cybersecurity to protect yourself and your digital assets in the ever-evolving digital landscape.

Introduction

In today's digital age, where personal information is shared online more than ever before, the threat of identity theft looms large. Identity theft occurs when a malicious individual obtains and misuses someone else's personal information without their consent. This nefarious act can have severe consequences for victims, including financial loss, damaged credit scores, and emotional distress. In this article, we will delve into the world of identity theft, exploring its various forms, common tactics employed by perpetrators, and strategies to protect yourself from falling prey to these digital imposters.

Understanding Identity Theft

Identity theft is a broad term that encompasses a range of fraudulent activities aimed at stealing personal information. From financial data to social security numbers, cybercriminals seek to exploit any piece of data that can be monetized or used to impersonate individuals. It is crucial to be aware of the different types of identity theft to effectively safeguard ourselves against these threats.

Types of Identity Theft

1. Financial Identity Theft

Financial identity theft is one of the most prevalent forms of identity theft. Criminals gain access to victims' financial information, such as credit card details or bank account numbers, to make unauthorized purchases or drain bank accounts. This can leave victims facing substantial financial losses and a lengthy process to recover their funds.

2. Social Security Identity Theft

Social security identity theft occurs when someone steals another person's social security number (SSN) to obtain employment, commit tax fraud, or apply for government benefits. The misuse of SSNs can have serious consequences, including tax liabilities and damaged credit histories.

3. Medical Identity Theft

Medical identity theft involves the fraudulent use of someone's personal information to obtain medical services, prescription drugs, or insurance reimbursements. Aside from financial implications, victims of medical identity theft may experience potential harm to their health due to inaccurate medical records and incorrect treatments administered based on stolen information.

4. Child Identity Theft

Child identity theft is a particularly distressing form of identity theft. Criminals exploit the clean credit histories of children, using their social security numbers to open fraudulent accounts or secure loans. As a result, children may face significant financial difficulties when they come of age, completely unaware of the theft until then.

Tactics Employed by Identity Thieves

1. Phishing

Phishing is a deceptive tactic used by identity thieves to trick individuals into divulging their sensitive information. This is often done through fraudulent emails, messages, or websites that appear legitimate, luring victims into providing personal data such as usernames, passwords, or credit card details.

2. Data Breaches

Data breaches occur when cybercriminals gain unauthorized access to a company's or organization's databases, obtaining a vast amount of personal information from multiple individuals. This stolen data is then sold on the black market or used for various fraudulent activities.

3. Skimming

Skimming involves the use of devices that capture credit or debit card information when individuals use them for transactions. Criminals attach these devices to ATMs, gas pumps, or other payment terminals to obtain card data, which they later use for unauthorized purchases or to create counterfeit cards.

Protecting Yourself from Identity Theft

1. Safeguard Your Personal Information

Be cautious about sharing personal information online. Only provide sensitive details on secure websites, and avoid sharing too much on social media platforms.

Regularly monitor your financial statements and credit reports for any suspicious activity.

2. Strengthen Your Passwords

Create strong, unique passwords for each of your online accounts. Use a combination of letters, numbers, and symbols, and avoid using easily guessable information such as your name or birthdate. Consider using a reputable password manager to securely store your passwords.

3. Be Wary of Phishing Attempts

Exercise caution when clicking on links or opening attachments in emails, especially if they appear suspicious or come from unknown senders. Avoid providing personal information or login credentials through email or unfamiliar websites.

4. Enable Two-Factor Authentication

Two-factor authentication adds an extra layer of security to your online accounts. By requiring a second form of verification, such as a code sent to your mobile device, even if your password is compromised, it becomes significantly harder for hackers to gain unauthorized access.

5. Regularly Update Your Software

Keep your operating system, antivirus software, and other applications up to date. Software updates often include security patches that protect against known vulnerabilities, reducing the risk of unauthorized access to your devices and personal information.

Conclusion

Identity theft is a pervasive and ever-evolving threat in the digital landscape. By understanding the various types of identity theft, familiarizing ourselves with the tactics employed by criminals, and implementing proactive measures to protect our personal information, we can significantly reduce the risk of falling victim to these digital imposters. Stay vigilant, educate yourself and your loved ones, and prioritize cybersecurity to safeguard your identity in today's interconnected world.

Introduction

In today's interconnected world, where information is readily accessible and technology is deeply ingrained in our lives, cyber threats have become increasingly sophisticated. While firewalls, antivirus software, and encryption algorithms are effective in defending against technical vulnerabilities, cybercriminals have found a new and effective method to breach security systems: social engineering. Social engineering exploits the human element, manipulating individuals to gain unauthorized access or obtain sensitive information. In this article, we will explore the concept of social engineering, its techniques, and the importance of awareness and education in defending against such attacks.

Understanding Social Engineering

Social engineering is a form of psychological manipulation that deceives individuals into revealing confidential information or performing actions that may compromise security. It preys on human vulnerabilities such as trust, curiosity, and fear. By exploiting these emotions, social engineers manipulate victims into divulging sensitive data, granting unauthorized access, or carrying out harmful actions.

Techniques of Social Engineering

1. Phishing

Phishing is one of the most common techniques used in social engineering attacks. Attackers impersonate trusted entities, such as banks or popular websites, and send fraudulent emails or messages to unsuspecting victims. These messages often contain urgent requests to verify personal information or click on malicious links, leading to the compromise of sensitive data or the installation of malware.

2. Pretexting

Pretexting involves creating a false narrative or scenario to gain someone's trust. Social engineers may pose as trusted individuals, such as technical support personnel, law enforcement officers, or colleagues, to extract sensitive information. They build credibility by researching their targets and using the acquired information to convince victims of their legitimacy.

3. Baiting

Baiting exploits human curiosity by offering something desirable in exchange for personal information or system access. It often involves leaving infected physical media, such as USB drives or CDs, in public places or workplaces, hoping that someone will pick them up and connect them to their devices. Once connected, the malware on the media can infiltrate the victim's system.

4. Tailgating

Tailgating, also known as piggybacking, occurs when an unauthorized individual gains access to a restricted area by closely following an authorized person. This technique relies on the assumption that people are generally helpful and hesitate to confront someone who appears to belong in the vicinity. Once inside, the social engineer can exploit the gained access for nefarious purposes.

The Importance of Awareness and Education

1. Recognizing Warning Signs

Raising awareness about social engineering attacks is crucial in combating them effectively. Individuals should be educated about the warning signs of a social engineering attempt, such as unsolicited requests for personal information, urgent or threatening messages, or suspicious behavior from unknown individuals.

2. Training and Simulations

Organizations should provide regular training sessions and simulations to their employees to enhance their understanding of social engineering tactics. By simulating real-world scenarios, employees can develop the skills to identify and respond appropriately to social engineering attempts, minimizing the risk of successful attacks.

3. Implementing Multifactor Authentication

To reduce the impact of stolen credentials, implementing multifactor authentication (MFA) is vital. MFA adds an extra layer of security by requiring additional verification steps, such as a fingerprint or a one-time password. This mitigates the risk of unauthorized access even if credentials are compromised through social engineering techniques.

4. Establishing a Security-Conscious Culture

Creating a security-conscious culture within organizations is essential. Encouraging employees to report suspicious incidents, implementing strong password policies, regularly updating software, and conducting security audits help build a robust defense against social engineering attacks.

Conclusion

Social engineering leverages human psychology to bypass technical defenses, making it a potent threat in the cyber landscape. Understanding the techniques employed by social engineers and promoting awareness and education among individuals and organizations are crucial in defending against these attacks. By fostering a security-conscious culture and implementing effective countermeasures, we can protect ourselves and our valuable information from the manipulative tactics of social engineering.

Introduction

In the digital age, the Internet has brought countless opportunities for communication, business, and personal growth. However, it has also opened the door to a darker side of human nature – online scams. From romance scams that prey on vulnerability to investment frauds that exploit financial aspirations, these scams have become increasingly prevalent in recent years. This article aims to shed light on the various types of online scams and provide readers with valuable insights to protect themselves in the digital realm.

The Rise of Online Scams

The proliferation of technology and the increasing interconnectedness of our lives have made it easier for scammers to find unsuspecting victims. With the anonymity provided by the Internet, scammers can create elaborate personas and manipulate individuals for personal gain. From fake social media profiles to fraudulent websites, scammers have become adept at deceiving people across various platforms.

Romance Scams: Playing with Emotions

Romance scams exploit the vulnerability and desire for companionship of individuals seeking love or friendship online. Scammers create fake profiles on dating websites or social media platforms, gaining the trust and affection of their victims before manipulating them into sending money. These scams often involve emotional manipulation, with scammers using tactics like feigning love, creating elaborate stories, or even faking emergencies to extort money from their victims.

Phishing Scams: Hook, Line, and Sinker

Phishing scams involve tricking individuals into revealing sensitive information such as passwords, credit card details, or personal identification. Scammers often pose as legitimate organizations, sending emails or messages that appear genuine, and luring recipients into clicking on malicious links or providing confidential information. These scams can lead to identity theft, financial loss, and even unauthorized access to personal accounts.

Investment Frauds: Promises of Wealth

Online investment scams appeal to individuals' desire to make quick and substantial profits. These scams often involve promises of high returns with little risk, enticing victims to invest in fraudulent schemes or non-existent ventures. Scammers may use fake investment websites, testimonials, or even manipulate online trading platforms to convince victims of their legitimacy. Unfortunately, victims often realize the deceit only after losing their hard-earned money.

Auction and Online Shopping Scams: A False Bargain

Auction and online shopping scams exploit the trust placed in online marketplaces. Scammers create fake listings, offering popular items at attractive prices to lure unsuspecting buyers. Victims may pay for the item but never receive it, or they might receive counterfeit or inferior products. These scams exploit the convenience of online shopping while preying on individuals' eagerness to find good deals.

Lottery and Sweepstakes Scams: Illusory Winnings

Lottery and sweepstakes scams deceive individuals by claiming they have won a large sum of money or valuable prizes. Scammers may contact victims via email, phone calls, or text messages, stating that they need to pay a fee or provide personal information to claim their winnings. In reality, there is no prize, and victims end up losing money or becoming victims of identity theft.

Tips to Protect Yourself

Be skeptical: Exercise caution when dealing with strangers online and be skeptical of offers that seem too good to be true.

Verify before trusting: Verify the legitimacy of individuals, organizations, or websites before sharing personal information or making financial commitments.

Protect your personal information: Never share sensitive information, such as passwords or financial details, through email or unfamiliar websites.

Stay updated: Regularly update your computer's antivirus software and keep yourself informed about the latest scams and security measures.

Report and seek help: If you encounter or fall victim to an online scam, report it to the appropriate authorities and seek assistance from your local law enforcement agency.

Conclusion

Online scams continue to evolve and exploit the vulnerabilities of unsuspecting individuals. By understanding the various types of scams and adopting preventive measures, we can protect ourselves and our loved ones from falling victim to these digital frauds. Remember, staying informed, skeptical, and cautious is crucial in navigating the digital landscape and ensuring a safer online experience for all.

Introduction

In today's interconnected world, the threat of malware attacks looms larger than ever. Cybercriminals are constantly devising new strategies to exploit vulnerabilities in our digital systems, wreaking havoc on individuals, businesses, and even governments. These malicious actors seek to profit from their nefarious activities, often targeting unsuspecting victims for financial gain. This article delves into the realm of malware attacks, shedding light on how vulnerabilities are exploited for profit, and the measures we can take to protect ourselves.

Understanding Malware

Malware, short for malicious software, encompasses a wide range of harmful programs designed to infiltrate, damage, or gain unauthorized access to computer systems. From viruses and worms to ransomware and spyware, malware poses significant threats to individuals and organizations alike. Cybercriminals employ various techniques to distribute malware, including email attachments, infected websites, malicious downloads, and social engineering tactics.

Exploiting Vulnerabilities

1. Software Vulnerabilities

Software vulnerabilities serve as entry points for malware attacks. Hackers meticulously search for weaknesses in operating systems, applications, and plugins, allowing them to exploit these flaws to gain control over targeted systems. Exploiting vulnerabilities such as outdated software, unpatched security flaws, or zero-day vulnerabilities enables attackers to gain unauthorized access, steal sensitive data, or disrupt operations.

2. Social Engineering

Cybercriminals often exploit the weakest link in any security system – the human element. Through social engineering tactics, such as phishing emails, deceptive phone calls, or impersonation, attackers manipulate individuals into revealing confidential information or clicking on malicious links. By leveraging human trust and emotions, hackers gain access to systems, facilitating the spread of malware.

Motives Behind Malware Attacks

1. Financial Gain

One of the primary motivations for malware attacks is financial profit. Cybercriminals employ various tactics, including ransomware attacks, banking trojans, and cryptocurrency mining malware, to extort money or steal valuable financial information. Ransomware encrypts victims' data, demanding a ransom payment for its release, while banking trojans target online banking credentials to siphon funds. Cryptocurrency mining malware hijacks victims' computing power to mine digital currencies without their knowledge.

2. Espionage and Intellectual Property Theft

State-sponsored cybercriminals and corporate spies often deploy sophisticated malware attacks to gather sensitive information, gain a competitive advantage, or disrupt rival organizations. Intellectual property theft can cause severe financial losses and undermine innovation in industries ranging from technology to defense.

3. Disruption and Extortion

Some malware attacks are motivated by causing chaos and disruption. Distributed Denial of Service (DDoS) attacks, for example, flood targeted systems with an overwhelming amount of traffic, rendering them inaccessible. Cybercriminals may launch DDoS attacks to extort money from organizations, threaten competitors, or disrupt critical infrastructure.

Protecting Against Malware Attacks

1. Keep Software Updated

Regularly updating operating systems, applications, and plugins is crucial for closing security vulnerabilities and protecting against known exploits. Enable automatic updates whenever possible and ensure that security patches are promptly installed.

2. Implement Strong Security Measures

Employ robust security measures, including firewalls, antivirus software, and intrusion detection systems, to detect and block malware threats. Consider using advanced security solutions that provide real-time protection, behavior analysis, and sandboxing capabilities to identify and neutralize emerging malware.

3. Educate and Train Users

Educating employees and individuals about the risks of malware attacks is paramount. Regular training sessions on identifying phishing attempts, safe browsing practices, and password hygiene can significantly reduce the likelihood of successful attacks.

4. Implement Multi-Factor Authentication

By requiring additional verification steps beyond passwords, such as biometric scans or one-time codes, multi-factor authentication adds an extra layer of security. This measure makes it harder for cybercriminals to gain unauthorized access, even if they manage to obtain users' credentials.

5. Regular Data Backups

Conducting regular backups of critical data is crucial in mitigating the impact of ransomware attacks. Ensure that backups are stored securely and independently from the primary system, minimizing the chances of data loss and enabling swift recovery.

Conclusion

Malware attacks continue to evolve in complexity and scale, posing significant threats to individuals, organizations, and societies at large. Cybercriminals exploit vulnerabilities in software and human behavior to achieve financial gain, espionage, or disruption. By staying vigilant, employing robust security measures, and implementing proactive strategies, we can fortify our defenses against these attacks. Safeguarding our digital systems and raising awareness about the risks of malware are essential steps towards a more secure digital future.

Introduction

In recent years, ransomware attacks have emerged as one of the most significant cyber threats facing individuals, businesses, and even governments. This malicious form of cybercrime has the potential to disrupt critical infrastructure, compromise sensitive data, and cause substantial financial losses. In this article, we will delve into the world of ransomware, exploring its origins, impact, and most importantly, the defense mechanisms that can be employed to mitigate the risk.

Understanding Ransomware

Ransomware is a type of malware that encrypts files and systems, rendering them inaccessible to the victim. The attacker then demands a ransom, usually in the form of cryptocurrency, in exchange for providing the decryption key. This insidious form of cyberattack has gained popularity among criminals due to its effectiveness and lucrative nature.

Origins and Evolution of Ransomware

Ransomware traces its roots back to the late 1980s when the first instances of encryption-based attacks were observed. However, it wasn't until the early 2000s that ransomware started to gain prominence with the emergence of encryption algorithms that were difficult to crack. Since then, ransomware has evolved significantly, with attackers constantly developing new techniques to exploit vulnerabilities in computer systems and networks.

Impact and Consequences

The impact of ransomware attacks can be devastating for individuals and organizations alike. For businesses, the temporary or permanent loss of critical data can lead to significant financial losses, reputation damage, and even legal implications. In the case of healthcare institutions or government agencies, the consequences can extend beyond financial losses and affect public safety and national security.

Common Infection Vectors

Ransomware can infiltrate systems through various infection vectors. Some of the most common methods employed by attackers include:

1. Phishing Emails: Attackers often use deceptive emails to trick users into downloading malicious attachments or clicking on infected links, allowing the ransomware to enter the system.

2. Malvertising: Malicious advertisements displayed on legitimate websites can contain hidden ransomware that infects systems when clicked.

3. Exploit Kits: These are pre-packaged software tools that identify and exploit vulnerabilities in outdated software, allowing ransomware to gain unauthorized access to systems.

4. Remote Desktop Protocol (RDP) Attacks: Attackers can exploit weak or unprotected RDP connections to gain unauthorized access to systems and deploy ransomware.

Defense Mechanisms

Prevention and preparedness are crucial when it comes to defending against ransomware attacks. Here are some effective defense mechanisms:

1. Employee Education: Training employees on recognizing phishing emails, suspicious links, and the importance of strong passwords can significantly reduce the risk of a successful ransomware attack.

2. Regular Software Updates: Keeping all software and operating systems up to date ensures that known vulnerabilities are patched, making it harder for attackers to exploit them.

3. Data Backups: Regularly backing up critical data and storing it offline or in secure, isolated networks can help restore systems without paying the ransom.

4. Network Segmentation: Dividing networks into smaller segments with restricted access can limit the spread of ransomware in the event of an attack, minimizing damage.

5. Robust Endpoint Security: Implementing strong antivirus and anti-malware solutions, along with intrusion detection systems, can detect and block ransomware before it can do harm.

6. Incident Response Plan: Having a well-defined incident response plan in place helps organizations respond effectively to a ransomware attack, minimizing downtime and reducing the impact.

The Role of Cybersecurity Professionals

Cybersecurity professionals play a critical role in combating the menace of ransomware. Their expertise in implementing and managing security measures, monitoring networks for suspicious activity, and promptly responding to incidents can significantly enhance an organization's resilience against ransomware attacks.

Conclusion

As ransomware attacks continue to evolve in sophistication and scale, it is essential for individuals, businesses, and governments to stay vigilant and take proactive measures to defend against this growing menace. By understanding the origins and impact of ransomware, implementing robust defense mechanisms, and fostering a culture of cybersecurity, we can collectively combat this cyber threat and safeguard our digital assets.

Introduction

In today's interconnected world, data breaches have become a serious concern for individuals, businesses, and governments alike. The increasing reliance on technology and the vast amounts of personal and sensitive information being stored online have made data breaches a pervasive threat. This article aims to shed light on the significance of data breaches, their causes, impacts, and the measures that can be taken to protect against such breaches.

Understanding Data Breaches

Data breaches refer to unauthorized access, disclosure, or acquisition of confidential or sensitive information. These incidents can occur due to various factors, including cyber attacks, human error, or system vulnerabilities. Hackers and cybercriminals target organizations to gain access to valuable data, such as personal identifiable information (PII), financial records, intellectual property, or trade secrets.

Causes of Data Breaches

1. Cyber Attacks

Cybercriminals employ sophisticated techniques like phishing, malware, ransomware, or SQL injections to exploit vulnerabilities in systems and networks. They aim to infiltrate databases and extract sensitive information for financial gain or malicious intent.

2. Human Error

Accidental actions by employees, such as sending sensitive data to the wrong recipient or falling victim to social engineering tactics, can lead to data breaches. Inadequate training, negligence, or lack of awareness contribute to such errors.

3. System Vulnerabilities

Outdated software, unpatched vulnerabilities, weak access controls, or misconfigured security settings create opportunities for cybercriminals to exploit and gain unauthorized access to sensitive data.

Impacts of Data Breaches

1. Financial Loss

Data breaches can lead to significant financial losses for organizations due to legal liabilities, regulatory fines, remediation costs, and reputational damage. The aftermath of a breach often involves legal battles, compensation claims, and a decline in customer trust.

2. Privacy Invasion

Individuals affected by data breaches face the risk of their personal information being exposed, leading to identity theft, fraud, or blackmail. This invasion of privacy can cause emotional distress and have long-term consequences for victims.

3. Reputational Damage

Organizations that fail to adequately protect customer data suffer reputational damage, leading to a loss of trust among existing and potential customers. Rebuilding a tarnished reputation can be a challenging and time-consuming task.

Preventive Measures

1. Strong Security Infrastructure

Organizations must establish robust security measures, including firewalls, encryption, intrusion detection systems, and multifactor authentication. Regular security audits and penetration testing help identify and address vulnerabilities proactively.

2. Employee Education and Awareness

Comprehensive training programs should be implemented to educate employees about data security best practices. This includes awareness about phishing emails, password hygiene, and proper handling of sensitive information.

3. Data Minimization and Encryption

Organizations should adopt a data minimization approach, collecting only the necessary information and storing it securely. Encryption techniques should be employed to protect data at rest and in transit, rendering it useless even if breached.

4. Incident Response Plan

Having a well-defined incident response plan in place allows organizations to respond swiftly and effectively to a data breach. This includes identifying the breach, containing it, notifying affected individuals, and implementing measures to prevent future incidents.

The Role of Legislation

Governments around the world have introduced data protection laws to hold organizations accountable for safeguarding personal information. Legislation, such as the General Data Protection Regulation (GDPR) and the California Consumer Privacy Act (CCPA), imposes strict requirements for data handling, breach reporting, and user consent.

Conclusion

Data breaches pose significant threats to individuals and organizations, undermining privacy, financial stability, and reputation. Understanding the causes and impacts of data breaches is crucial for implementing effective preventive measures. By adopting strong security practices, educating employees, minimizing data collection, and adhering to relevant legislation, organizations can reinforce their defenses and mitigate the risks associated with data breaches. Only by adopting a proactive and comprehensive approach can we strengthen the fortress of information and safeguard our valuable data from malicious attacks.

Introduction

In today's interconnected world, financial frauds have become increasingly sophisticated, posing a significant threat to individuals, businesses, and even governments. With the rapid advancement of technology, cybercriminals have found new avenues to exploit vulnerabilities and deceive unsuspecting victims. To protect yourself and your assets, it is crucial to understand the web of deception woven by these fraudsters. In this article, we will delve into the world of financial frauds and explore strategies to empower yourself against cyber crimes and frauds.

The Rising Tide of Financial Frauds

Financial frauds have experienced an alarming surge in recent years, fueled by technological advancements and the proliferation of online transactions. Cybercriminals employ various tactics to deceive individuals, ranging from identity theft and phishing scams to investment frauds and Ponzi schemes. The impact of these frauds can be devastating, leading to significant financial losses, reputational damage, and emotional distress.

Understanding the Mindset of Fraudsters

To effectively protect ourselves against financial frauds, it is essential to gain insights into the mindset of fraudsters. Fraudsters often exploit psychological vulnerabilities, such as greed, fear, and trust, to manipulate their victims. By understanding these tactics, individuals can develop a healthy skepticism and critical thinking approach when faced with suspicious offers or requests for personal information.

Types of Financial Frauds

1. Identity Theft: One of the most prevalent forms of financial fraud is identity theft. Cybercriminals steal personal information, such as Social Security numbers and financial account details, to commit fraudulent activities. They may open credit accounts, make unauthorized purchases, or even drain bank accounts, leaving victims in financial ruin.

2. Phishing Scams: Phishing scams involve fraudulent emails, text messages, or websites that appear to be from legitimate sources, tricking individuals into revealing sensitive information like passwords or credit card details. These scams often create a sense of urgency or exploit current events to deceive unsuspecting victims.

3. Investment Fraud: Investment frauds lure victims with promises of high returns or exclusive investment opportunities. Ponzi schemes, pyramid schemes, and fraudulent initial coin offerings (ICOs) are examples of investment frauds where individuals are enticed to invest their hard-earned money, only to have it disappear into the hands of fraudsters.

Protecting Yourself Against Financial Frauds

1. Strengthening Online Security: Protecting your online presence is crucial in the fight against financial frauds. Use strong, unique passwords for each online account, enable multi-factor authentication, and keep your devices and software up to date with the latest security patches. Additionally, be cautious when sharing personal

information online and avoid clicking on suspicious links or downloading files from unknown sources.

2. Enhancing Financial Literacy: **Educating yourself about personal finance and investment principles can provide a solid foundation to recognize and avoid fraudulent schemes. Understand the basics of investing, research before making financial decisions, and consult reputable financial advisors when needed. Remember, if an investment opportunity seems too good to be true, it probably is.**

3. Developing Healthy Skepticism: **Cultivate a healthy skepticism when approached with unsolicited offers or requests for personal information. Verify the authenticity of individuals and organizations before sharing sensitive details. Be cautious of high-pressure tactics that create a sense of urgency or secrecy, as fraudsters often exploit these emotions to manipulate their victims.**

4. Monitoring Financial Activities: **Regularly monitor your financial accounts for any unauthorized transactions or suspicious activities. Review bank statements, credit card bills, and credit reports for discrepancies. Promptly report any suspected fraud to your financial institutions to mitigate potential losses.**

5. Reporting Fraudulent Activities: **Reporting financial fraud is essential to protect others from falling victim to the same schemes. Contact your local law enforcement agencies and report the incident to organizations such as the Federal Trade Commission (FTC) or the Internet Crime Complaint Center (IC3).**

Conclusion

Financial frauds continue to pose a significant threat in today's digital landscape. By understanding the tactics employed by fraudsters and implementing proactive measures, individuals can empower themselves against cyber crimes and frauds. Strengthening online security, enhancing financial literacy, cultivating healthy skepticism, monitoring financial activities, and reporting fraudulent incidents are essential steps to safeguarding oneself against the web of deception. Together, we can create a safer environment and protect our financial well-being in the digital age.

Introduction

In today's digital age, the internet has become an integral part of our lives. It has opened up new avenues for communication, learning, and entertainment. However, with these advancements come certain risks, one of which is cyberstalking and harassment. Cyberstalking refers to the act of using digital platforms to harass, intimidate, or threaten an individual. It can have serious consequences for the victim's mental and emotional well-being. In this article, we will explore the various aspects of cyberstalking and harassment and discuss effective ways to protect personal privacy in the digital realm.

Understanding Cyberstalking and Harassment

Cyberstalking can take many forms, including sending unwanted messages or emails, spreading false rumors, stalking social media profiles, and even hacking into someone's accounts. It is a distressing experience for the victims, as they constantly feel violated and unsafe. Harassment, on the other hand, involves persistent unwanted behavior that causes fear, annoyance, or distress. These acts can have severe psychological effects, leading to anxiety, depression, and even suicidal thoughts in extreme cases.

The Importance of Personal Privacy

Personal privacy is crucial in the digital world, where our personal information is often stored and shared online. Maintaining privacy helps protect our identities, prevent identity theft, and safeguard our personal and professional relationships. It is essential to be mindful of the information we share and take proactive measures to ensure our privacy.

Protecting Personal Privacy

1. Secure Online Presence: It is vital to regularly update privacy settings on social media platforms to control who can view and access your personal information. Be cautious about accepting friend requests from unknown individuals and limit the amount of personal information you share publicly.

2. Strong Passwords and Two-Factor Authentication: Using strong, unique passwords for each online account can significantly enhance your privacy. Additionally, enabling two-factor authentication adds an extra layer of security by requiring a second verification step, such as a code sent to your mobile device.

3. Avoid Clicking Suspicious Links: Phishing attacks are common methods used by cyberstalkers to gain unauthorized access to personal information. Be cautious of unsolicited emails or messages containing suspicious links, and avoid clicking on them. Verify the legitimacy of the source before taking any action.

4. Be Mindful of Location Sharing: Many mobile apps and social media platforms allow users to share their location with others. While this feature can be useful, it can also compromise personal privacy. Consider disabling location sharing or restricting it to trusted individuals only.

5. Regularly Monitor Online Presence: Keep a close eye on your digital footprint by searching for your name online

and monitoring your social media accounts. Report and block any instances of harassment or cyberstalking promptly.

Legal Recourse for Cyberstalking and Harassment

If you become a victim of cyberstalking or harassment, it is important to know your legal rights and seek appropriate recourse. Laws regarding cyberstalking vary by jurisdiction, but many countries have implemented legislation to address this issue. Document all instances of harassment and report them to the relevant authorities. Preserve evidence such as screenshots, emails, and messages to support your case.

Support and Seek Professional Help

Dealing with cyberstalking and harassment can be emotionally draining, and it is crucial to seek support from friends, family, or professionals. Talk to someone you trust about your experiences and feelings. If the situation escalates or becomes unbearable, consider reaching out to law enforcement agencies, online platforms, or organizations that specialize in combating cyberstalking and harassment.

Conclusion

Cyberstalking and harassment are unfortunate consequences of our increasingly interconnected world. It is crucial to be aware of the risks and take proactive steps to protect personal privacy online. By securing our online presence, using strong passwords, being cautious of suspicious links, and seeking legal recourse when necessary, we can empower ourselves against cyberstalkers and create a safer digital environment. Remember, personal privacy matters, and taking a stand against cyberstalking is essential for the well-being and security of individuals in the online realm.

Introduction

In the digital age, the internet has become an integral part of our lives, connecting people from all around the world. While the internet has provided numerous benefits, it has also given rise to new forms of harassment and abuse, particularly in the form of cyberbullying. Cyberbullying refers to the use of digital communication platforms to intentionally harm, intimidate, or harass individuals. This article explores the phenomenon of cyberbullying and offers insights into how to navigate this treacherous terrain.

Understanding Cyberbullying

1. Defining Cyberbullying

Cyberbullying encompasses various forms of online abuse, including harassment, threats, spreading rumors, and exclusion. It can occur through social media platforms, instant messaging apps, online gaming platforms, and other digital spaces.

2. The Impact of Cyberbullying

Cyberbullying can have severe consequences for victims. It can lead to psychological distress, low self-esteem, anxiety, depression, and even suicidal ideation. Additionally, it affects academic performance, social relationships, and overall well-being.

3. Cyberbullying vs. Traditional Bullying

While traditional bullying typically takes place in person, cyberbullying transcends physical boundaries. It provides bullies with anonymity and an extended reach, intensifying the impact on victims. The viral nature of online content makes it difficult to escape the torment.

Types and Tactics of Cyberbullying

1. Harassment and Threats

Cyberbullies often engage in persistent harassment, sending offensive messages, threats, or even making public threats of physical harm. This type of cyberbullying can be traumatic and cause severe distress to victims.

2. Rumor Spreading

One prevalent tactic of cyberbullies is spreading false rumors or gossip about the victim. The viral nature of social media can quickly amplify these rumors, leading to reputational damage and social isolation.

3. Impersonation and Identity Theft

Cyberbullies may create fake profiles or impersonate others to deceive and manipulate their victims. They may steal personal information and use it to harass or embarrass individuals.

4. Exclusion and Online Shaming

Cyberbullies often engage in excluding individuals from online groups, intentionally leaving them out of conversations or activities. Additionally, online shaming involves publicly ridiculing and humiliating individuals through photos, videos, or derogatory comments.

Responding to Cyberbullying

1. Recognizing the Signs

It is crucial to be aware of the signs of cyberbullying, such as sudden changes in behavior, withdrawal from social activities, reluctance to use electronic devices, or emotional distress. Identifying these signs can help in taking timely action.

2. Documenting Evidence

Victims should document any instances of cyberbullying, including screenshots, messages, and timestamps. This evidence can be essential when reporting the abuse to authorities or online platforms.

3. Seeking Support

Victims of cyberbullying should reach out to trusted friends, family members, or professionals for emotional support. Organizations and helplines specializing in cyberbullying can provide guidance and assistance.

4. Reporting and Blocking

It is crucial to report cyberbullying incidents to the relevant social media platforms or websites. Most platforms have mechanisms in place to address abuse. Additionally, blocking the bully's account can help reduce further contact and harassment.

5. Promoting Digital Literacy and Online Safety

Educating individuals, especially children and adolescents, about digital literacy and online safety is vital. Teaching them to be cautious about sharing personal information and promoting responsible online behavior can help prevent cyberbullying.

Preventing Cyberbullying

1. Fostering a Culture of Respect

Creating a culture of respect and empathy both online and offline is crucial in preventing cyberbullying. Promoting kindness, tolerance, and acceptance can help cultivate an environment where cyberbullying is less likely to occur.

2. Parental and School Involvement

Parents and educators play a significant role in preventing and addressing cyberbullying. By monitoring online activities, engaging in open conversations, and implementing appropriate policies, they can create a safe digital environment for children.

3. Encouraging Bystander Intervention

Bystanders witnessing cyberbullying incidents can make a difference by intervening and supporting the victim. Encouraging individuals to speak out against cyberbullying helps create a collective effort to combat this issue.

Conclusion

Cyberbullying is a distressing reality in the digital age. Understanding the various forms of cyberbullying, recognizing the signs, and taking appropriate action are essential in navigating this digital abuse terrain. By fostering a culture of respect, promoting digital literacy, and encouraging intervention, we can strive to create a safer and more compassionate online world for everyone.

Exploring the Hidden Underbelly of the Internet

Introduction

The internet has transformed the way we communicate, access information, and conduct business. It has connected people from all corners of the globe and has become an integral part of our daily lives. However, beneath the surface of the visible internet lies a mysterious and clandestine world known as the dark web. In this article, we will delve into the dark web, its workings, and the unique challenges it presents.

What is the Dark Web?

The dark web is a hidden part of the internet that can only be accessed through special software or configurations, providing anonymity to its users. It is a network of websites that are not indexed by search engines and are intentionally concealed from the public eye. While the visible internet, known as the surface web, comprises a small portion of the entire internet, the dark web is estimated to be significantly larger.

The Onion Routing and Anonymity

One of the key technologies that power the dark web is Tor (The Onion Router). Tor is a free and open-source software that enables anonymous communication by relaying internet traffic through a network of volunteer-operated servers. This process, called onion routing, encrypts and redirects data multiple times, making it extremely difficult to trace back to its source. The anonymity provided by Tor has made it a popular tool for activists, whistleblowers, journalists, and individuals seeking privacy.

Marketplaces and Illicit Activities

The dark web has gained notoriety for being a hub of illegal activities. Online marketplaces operating on the dark web facilitate the buying and selling of drugs, weapons, counterfeit goods, stolen data, and various other illicit products and services. Cryptocurrencies like Bitcoin are often used as the preferred method of payment, providing a layer of anonymity to transactions. While not all activities on the dark web are illegal, its anonymity has made it an attractive platform for criminals.

Cybersecurity Threats and Hacking Forums

The dark web harbors numerous hacking forums where cybercriminals exchange tools, techniques, and stolen data. These forums pose a significant cybersecurity threat, as hackers collaborate and share knowledge to carry out attacks on individuals, organizations, and even governments. The stolen data, including personal information, credit card details, and login credentials, is often sold on these forums, leading to identity theft and financial loss.

Whistleblowing and Freedom of Speech

While the dark web is frequently associated with criminal activities, it also serves as a platform for whistleblowers and activists operating in repressive regimes. The anonymity provided by the dark web enables individuals to share sensitive information without fear of reprisal. It has been instrumental in exposing corruption, human rights abuses, and government surveillance, providing a lifeline for those seeking to challenge oppressive regimes and protect freedom of speech.

Law Enforcement Challenges

The nature of the dark web poses significant challenges for law enforcement agencies worldwide. Its decentralized and anonymous nature makes it difficult to track and apprehend criminals. However, over the years, law enforcement agencies have made significant strides in combating illegal activities on the dark web. Coordinated international operations have led to the takedown of prominent dark web marketplaces and the arrest of high-profile criminals.

Ethical Considerations and Controversies

The dark web raises complex ethical considerations. On one hand, it provides a platform for whistleblowers, activists, and individuals seeking privacy in an increasingly surveilled world. On the other hand, it enables illegal activities, facilitating the sale of drugs, weapons, and stolen data. The debate surrounding the dark web centers on striking a balance between protecting privacy and ensuring public safety.

Conclusion

The dark web remains an enigma, holding both promise and peril. While it serves as a refuge for those seeking privacy and freedom of speech, it also harbors criminal activities that pose significant threats to individuals and societies. As technology continues to evolve, it is crucial to address the challenges posed by the dark web while protecting the principles of privacy and freedom that underpin the functioning of the internet.

Introduction

In an increasingly interconnected world, our digital lives are constantly exposed to various cyber threats. Cyber crimes and frauds have become more sophisticated and widespread, targeting individuals, businesses, and even governments. It is crucial for everyone to empower themselves with cybersecurity best practices to protect their digital assets and personal information. This article will provide you with valuable insights and practical tips on how to safeguard your digital life.

Understanding Cybersecurity Risks

Cyber threats can take various forms, including malware, phishing attacks, data breaches, ransomware, and identity theft. It is essential to recognize the potential risks involved and stay informed about the latest trends in cybercrime. Awareness is the first step towards protecting yourself effectively.

Strong Passwords and Authentication

Creating strong and unique passwords is fundamental to secure your online accounts. Avoid using common phrases or personal information and instead opt for a combination of uppercase and lowercase letters, numbers, and special characters. Furthermore, consider implementing two-factor authentication (2FA) wherever possible, as it adds an extra layer of security.

Regular Software Updates

Keeping your operating system, applications, and antivirus software up to date is crucial. Developers constantly release updates to patch security vulnerabilities. Ignoring these updates can leave your devices and personal information susceptible to attacks. Enable automatic updates whenever possible to ensure you are protected against the latest threats.

Be Cautious of Phishing Attempts

Phishing emails and messages are a common method used by cybercriminals to deceive users and gain access to their sensitive information. Be vigilant when opening emails, especially those from unknown sources. Avoid clicking on suspicious links or downloading attachments from untrusted senders. Verify the authenticity of any request for personal information before sharing it.

Secure Wi-Fi Networks

Public Wi-Fi networks can be a breeding ground for cybercriminals. Avoid connecting to unsecured or unknown Wi-Fi networks, particularly when handling sensitive information. When using public Wi-Fi, consider using a virtual private network (VPN) to encrypt your internet connection and protect your data from potential eavesdropping.

Data Backup and Encryption

Regularly backing up your important data is crucial in case of a cyber attack or hardware failure. Use secure cloud storage or external hard drives to store your backups. Additionally, encrypting sensitive data adds an extra layer of protection, making it unreadable to unauthorized individuals even if they gain access to it.

Social Media Privacy Settings

Review and adjust your social media privacy settings to control the visibility of your personal information. Limit the amount of information you share publicly and be cautious about accepting friend requests or connecting with unknown individuals. Be mindful of the information you post and avoid sharing sensitive details that can be used against you.

Avoid Suspicious Websites and Downloads

Exercise caution when visiting websites or downloading files from the internet. Stick to reputable sources and be skeptical of offers that seem too good to be true. Malicious websites and downloads can contain malware that can compromise your device and personal information.

Cybersecurity Education and Awareness

Stay informed about the latest cybersecurity threats, trends, and best practices through reputable sources. Attend webinars, workshops, or online courses to enhance your knowledge and understanding of cybersecurity. Educate your family members, friends, and colleagues about the importance of cybersecurity and encourage them to adopt best practices.

Regular Monitoring and Reporting

Regularly monitor your financial accounts, credit reports, and online activities for any suspicious or unauthorized transactions. Report any cybercrime incidents to the appropriate authorities promptly. Timely reporting can help protect others from falling victim to the same fraud and increase the chances of catching the perpetrators.

Conclusion

In the digital age, safeguarding your digital life is a critical responsibility. By following these cybersecurity best practices, you can significantly reduce the risk of falling victim to cyber crimes and frauds. Remember to stay vigilant, keep your software updated, use strong passwords, and be cautious of suspicious activities. Empower yourself with knowledge and take proactive steps to protect your digital assets, personal information, and online privacy. By doing so, you can navigate the digital world with confidence and peace of mind.

Introduction

In today's interconnected world, the rise of technology and the internet has brought numerous benefits and opportunities. However, it has also given rise to new challenges, particularly in the form of cybercrimes. With the increasing frequency and sophistication of cyber attacks, it has become imperative to establish a robust legal framework to combat these crimes effectively. This article explores the importance of a strong legal framework in the battle against cyber crimes and highlights key sub-heads such as defining cyber crimes, international cooperation, legislation, and enforcement.

Defining Cyber Crimes

Cyber crimes encompass a wide range of illegal activities conducted through digital means, including hacking, identity theft, online fraud, data breaches, and cyber terrorism. The first step in combating these crimes is to establish a clear and comprehensive definition of what constitutes a cyber crime. This definition should encompass various forms of malicious activities committed through computer networks, systems, or devices.

International Cooperation

Cyber crimes transcend national boundaries, making international cooperation crucial in combating them effectively. Cyber criminals often exploit jurisdictional challenges, utilizing servers in different countries and hiding their identities. To address this, governments and law enforcement agencies must work collaboratively to share information, intelligence, and expertise. International agreements and treaties play a significant role in facilitating such cooperation, enabling the extradition of cyber criminals and harmonizing legal approaches across jurisdictions.

Legislative Measures

To combat cyber crimes, countries need to enact appropriate legislation that addresses the unique challenges posed by the digital realm. Such legislation should provide clear guidelines on what constitutes a cyber crime, establish penalties, and outline procedures for investigation and prosecution. Additionally, it should focus on protecting the rights of victims and ensuring the privacy and security of individuals and organizations. Regular updates and revisions to these laws are essential to keep pace with rapidly evolving cyber threats.

Data Protection and Privacy Laws

Given the increasing amount of personal and sensitive information being stored and transmitted online, robust data protection and privacy laws are crucial in the battle against cyber crimes. These laws govern the collection, storage, and use of personal data by organizations and individuals, ensuring that appropriate security measures are in place. Adequate safeguards, such as encryption and anonymization, must be implemented to protect data from unauthorized access or misuse.

Cybersecurity Standards

A strong legal framework must include provisions for cybersecurity standards to be followed by both public and private entities. These standards outline best practices for securing digital infrastructure, protecting networks, and mitigating cyber threats. Governments and regulatory bodies should establish frameworks that promote cybersecurity awareness, risk management, and incident response. Regular audits and compliance assessments should be conducted to ensure that organizations adhere to these standards.

Law Enforcement and Judicial Capacity

Building the necessary law enforcement and judicial capacity is crucial to effectively combat cyber crimes. Specialized cybercrime units within law enforcement agencies should be established, equipped with the necessary tools, training, and expertise to investigate and respond to cyber threats. Similarly, judges and prosecutors need to receive specialized training to understand the technical aspects of cyber crimes and effectively adjudicate cases.

International Legal Assistance

Cyber crimes often require international cooperation in gathering evidence, apprehending suspects, and sharing intelligence. Mutual legal assistance treaties and agreements facilitate this process by establishing mechanisms for countries to request and provide legal assistance in cyber crime investigations and prosecutions. Streamlining and strengthening these channels of communication and cooperation are essential in the battle against cyber crimes.

Public Awareness and Education

Raising public awareness about cyber threats and promoting digital literacy are crucial components of any legal framework. Governments, educational institutions, and non-profit organizations should collaborate to develop and implement cybersecurity education programs. By equipping individuals with the knowledge and skills to protect themselves and their organizations from cyber crimes, we can create a more secure digital environment.

Conclusion

The battle against cyber crimes requires a robust legal framework that addresses the unique challenges posed by the digital realm. Defining cyber crimes, fostering international cooperation, enacting effective legislation, and building law enforcement and judicial capacity are essential steps in this journey. By prioritizing data protection, cybersecurity standards, and public awareness, we can collectively combat cyber crimes and create a safer digital world for all.

Introduction

In our increasingly digital world, the threat landscape is constantly evolving, and with it, the need for effective safeguards against cyber crimes and frauds. As technology advances, so do the methods and tactics employed by malicious actors. To empower ourselves against these emerging threats, it is crucial to stay informed about the latest trends in cybercrime and understand the technological safeguards that can protect us. In this article, we will explore some of the future trends in cyber threats and the corresponding technological measures that can help defend against them.

The Rise of Artificial Intelligence in Cyber Attacks

With the exponential growth of artificial intelligence (AI) and machine learning (ML), cybercriminals are leveraging these technologies to carry out sophisticated attacks. AI-powered attacks can automate tasks, adapt to changing environments, and exploit vulnerabilities at an unprecedented scale. This poses a significant challenge for traditional security systems that struggle to keep pace with evolving attack techniques.

Technological Safeguard: AI-Enhanced Security Systems

To combat AI-driven cyber attacks, the development of AI-enhanced security systems is crucial. These systems utilize advanced algorithms to detect and respond to threats in real-time. By employing machine learning and data analytics, these safeguards can identify anomalous patterns,

detect zero-day vulnerabilities, and proactively defend against AI-powered attacks.

Internet of Things (IoT) Vulnerabilities

The proliferation of IoT devices presents a vast attack surface for cybercriminals. These devices, ranging from smart home appliances to industrial control systems, often lack robust security measures. Exploiting vulnerabilities in IoT devices can lead to severe consequences, including unauthorized access to personal data, disruption of critical infrastructure, and even physical harm.

Technological Safeguard: Secure IoT Ecosystems

To mitigate IoT vulnerabilities, it is crucial to establish secure IoT ecosystems. This includes implementing strong encryption, authentication protocols, and regular firmware updates. Additionally, manufacturers must prioritize security in the design and development of IoT devices, ensuring that they have built-in security features and are regularly patched against emerging threats.

Ransomware and Extortion

Ransomware attacks have become a significant concern, with high-profile incidents affecting businesses, healthcare organizations, and even critical infrastructure. Cybercriminals employ sophisticated ransomware strains that encrypt valuable data and demand ransom payments in exchange for its release. These attacks can cause substantial financial losses and disrupt operations, highlighting the need for robust defenses.

Technological Safeguard: Behavioral Analysis and Incident Response

To defend against ransomware attacks, organizations should adopt proactive security measures. This includes deploying behavioral analysis systems that can detect ransomware activities in real-time, identify early indicators of compromise, and mitigate threats before they can cause significant damage. Additionally, organizations must establish effective incident response plans to minimize the impact of successful attacks and facilitate swift recovery.

Social Engineering and Phishing

While technological advancements are significant, human factors remain a critical element in cybercrime. Social engineering and phishing attacks continue to exploit human psychology and trust to deceive individuals and gain unauthorized access to sensitive information. These tactics often target unsuspecting users through emails, phone calls, or fraudulent websites.

Technological Safeguard: Security Awareness and Training

To combat social engineering and phishing attacks, it is essential to cultivate a culture of security awareness and provide comprehensive training to individuals. Educating users about the techniques employed by cybercriminals, teaching them how to identify suspicious emails or websites, and encouraging a skeptical mindset can significantly reduce the success rate of such attacks.

Conclusion

As the digital landscape evolves, so do the threats we face. Understanding the emerging trends in cybercrime and fraud is essential for empowering ourselves against these dangers. By embracing technological safeguards such as AI-enhanced security systems, secure IoT ecosystems, proactive incident response, and comprehensive security awareness, we can better protect ourselves and our organizations. In the face of relentless cyber threats, a proactive and informed approach is crucial to safeguarding our digital lives.

"Empower Yourself Against Cyber Crimes and Frauds" is a comprehensive guide that equips readers with the knowledge and strategies needed to navigate the treacherous world of cyber threats. With an in-depth exploration of various topics, including phishing, identity theft, social engineering, online scams, malware attacks, ransomware, data breaches, financial frauds, cyberstalking, cyberbullying, the dark web, cybersecurity best practices, the legal framework, and future trends, this book offers valuable insights into the modern cyber threat landscape. Packed with practical advice and defense mechanisms, this book is an indispensable resource for individuals looking to protect themselves and their digital lives from the ever-evolving dangers of cyber crimes and frauds.

ABOUT THE AUTHOR

Mr. C. P. Kumar is a retired Scientist 'G' from National Institute of Hydrology, Roorkee, Uttarakhand, India. He is also a Reiki Healer and Chakra Balancing practitioner (with pendulum dowsing) and offers Emotional Freedom Technique (EFT) to help individuals with emotional issues. Mr. Kumar has authored many books on technical, spiritual, and social topics.

For further details, you may visit his webpage
https://www.angelfire.com/nh/cpkumar/virgo.html